Professor Re Nie's

THE
SECRETS
OF
JIU JITSU

- with more than 30 illustrations -

PARIS 1905
LIBRAIRIE PAUL PACLOT
4 RUE CASSETTE, 4

Translated by M.P. Lynch

CONTENTS:

I. Jiu Jitsu Debuts in Paris
II. History of Jiu Jitsu
III. Preparatory Training
Nutrition
Breathing
Hygiene
Exercises
IV. Techniques:
Let's Go!
Twist the Hand
Send him over your head
Counter a choke
Counter a high knife attack
Counter a knife attack II
Counter a leg kick
Counter a punch
Arm lock
Pass under the attacking arm
Invert the hand
Attack the cervical vertebrae
Grounded armbar
Strangle with vertebral separation
Break the elbow with a knee
Break the elbow with your instep
Achilles lock
Break the neck

I.
Jiu Jitsu debuts in Paris

    It is not as if there were a dearth of great inventions arising from the Far East: The people of Asia invented the compass, the printing press, and gunpowder long before we knew of them. Imported into Europe almost by chance, which is most often the vehicle through which ideas are exchanged much like seeds upon the wind, these discoveries then took a relatively long time to germinate and produce those marvelous effects which have since become so commonplace to us. Many ideas required a long incubation period, or one might say a longer appropriation process, in order to take root within the new civilization through which they would evolve.

    Nonetheless, the compass, the printing press, and gunpowder have all revolutionized the world, and like these things *Jiu Jitsu* came to us from the East - indeed the farthest east possible, since the art was born in Japan. Will it change the world like those other great inventions?

    Such a proposition is as risky to confirm as it is to deny.

    The people of modern European societies are currently under pressure from two forces: The excessive refinement caused by intellectualism and materialism. Both of these aggravate our neuroses and produce physical weakness and/or psychosomatic symptoms, and both are the ultimate product, one active and the other passive, of our nervous overactivity.

    However, a salutary reaction against both of these plagues of modern western society can be found in the pursuit of sports, a remedy which has been espoused by many perspicacious physicians.

    Now if many are quick to disregard such advice and prefer to let themselves slide into a state where their nervous system becomes either inert or disordered, it may be because the majority of athletic activities currently on offer are not really designed for the masses. Many of them demand a long and brutal training process which might also prove expensive, and as such they are inaccessible to the physically weak and the impecunious - which is to say, to those who need them the most!

What if there were a sport which was easy to practice, elegant, intelligent, and within the reach of every budget? Why, such a sport would have a serious chance at taking root, developing, and even transforming modern life.

Jiu Jitsu is just such a sport!

Just yesterday it was unknown in the west. It was brought to the Occident by the terrible upheaval of the war in Manchuria. In England and America it made a timid appearance as a sort of curiosity rather than a serious pursuit. In France it made a splash at the exhibition match between Master-at-Arms Georges Dubois and Professor Re Nie in October of 1905.

Since that memorable date this strange name has drawn the attention of all, and now it has become a household word. You cannot find a Parisian or a provincial who does not recognize it, and there isn't a newspaper which has not featured it with praise or disdain, for as always the press never comes down on one side of an issue. This is in the interest of journalism - it would perish without the clash of contraries.

How to explain the sudden craze for *Jiu Jitsu* in France?

Let us give due credit to the French sensibility: It has an instinct for placing confidence where it is merited, and feeling in regards to *Jiu Jitsu*, despite the exotic name, has been that it is entirely in keeping with our national character.

Nothing is better at proving the worth of this art than that it has shown itself to be the most excellent form of self defense. It allows a weaker person to calmly grapple with and subdue a stronger, more violent person, while at the same time it builds health, is easy to practice, and costs little. It is also the most elegant of sports - a characteristic which is entirely in keeping with the French national character.

There have been so many Parisian fads which have burst on the scene in the manner of *Jiu Jitsu* only to fade because they are in essence superficial, and their time on the scene is the caprice of a moment.

This will never happen with *Jiu Jitsu*: It will abide with us alongside La Boxe Française and English Boxing. It will in time become one of the great sports globally, and there will come a time when it is familiar to all.

Law enforcement has been so receptive that since the Re Nié versus Dubois match a number of top agents have been sent to learn *Jiu Jitsu* at the dojo on the Rue Ponthieu. Hardly had the lawmen begun to train when they grasped the undeniable interest this sport holds, not only from the point of view of general knowledge and physical education, but even more from the perspective of the practical need officers have to defend their own lives and the lives of those the people they serve from the brutal attacks of criminals!

What was it about the Re Nié vs. Dubois encounter that engendered such fascination? Was it because it offered proof that *Jiu Jitsu* possessed the formidable power it was said to hold?

You need only read what is to follow in order to be convinced. The official report we are going to give regarding this fabled encounter must by its nature be placed at the head of this book, and it cannot be burdened with exaggeration as it has been in all of the many sporting magazines and journals aimed at physical training which have long spoken of the contest with praise for the victor - but that is not the point.

First let us look at the contenders:

Master-at-Arms Georges Dubois is a well known figure in Paris. He is both a renowned boxer and a swordsman of the first order. When it comes to expertise in weight training he has few equals. Born in 1865 he weighs about 75 kilos and measures 1 meter 68.

Thus he presented Re Nié with the most serious of adversaries, above all when one considers that this latter weighs a mere 63 kilos and stands only 1 meter 65. He is 36 years of age.

The encounter took place on the 26th of October near the Vedrine factory in Courbevoie before a crowd of more than 500 spectators drawn almost entirely from the sporting world. They thus comprised a body of expert judges in this field, and later they would bear impartial witness to the astonishing result of the match.

Mr. Manaud was the presiding official and was responsible for organizing the exhibition.

At 2:30 the contenders arrived, and both men were clad in normal street attire. Re Nié had removed his false collar.

The fight was not set to end until one of the contenders declared himself beaten.

At the command of *Let's go, gentlemen!* the contenders came out from opposite corners rather quickly, then stopped at 2 meters apart and watched one another for a few seconds.

Dubois attacked first with a low kick which Re Nié evaded before wrapping his adversary up around the body. Applying a knee skillfully under the opponent's right thigh, he used his left hand to draw Dubois' lower back into him resulting in a hard fall to the shoulderblades.

Re Nié went to ground with the opponent and, when seized by the throat, he took Dubois' right wrist and, turning onto his back to the right of the other man, he passed a leg over Dubois' neck to constrict the carotid artery. This done he, Re Nié pulled his opponent's arm violently such that it was cantilevered, and this hold made it easy to hyperextend the elbow. The pain Dubois experienced caused him to cry out after having resisted for a fraction of a second, and he declared himself beaten.

He'd been caught in one of the most terrible locks of *Jiu Jitsu* known as the *udi-shi-ghi* [ude hishigi juji gatame]. The encounter had lasted for 26 seconds, and the combat properly speaking was only 6 seconds.

When Dubois was released from the hold which Re Nié had relinquished so quickly when he heard his opponent cry out, he stood up and offered his hand to the *Jiu Jitsu* champion as the crowd pressed in around the fighters.

"I would have liked to have made a better showing," said Dubois, "but it was impossible to escape. Had I continued my arm would have been broken like a piece of straw."

This almost unbelievable victory left the spectators stunned. People began speculating, and the most extraordinary discourses were pursued.

"Dubois ought to have done this - or that - he should have blocked the attack as follows - he ought to have gone at it in this way..."

But without being asked Dubois frankly admitted: "There was nothing I could have done." More than one of the critics of his game would have been equally stymied had they been in his shoes.

For the rest, all of the commentary and noise, all of the shock generated by this event pointed to what a revolution the prompt result (witnessed only by sportsmen) would signify when it was touted in all of the Parisian sporting journals on the following day.

One could say that it had been definitively demonstrated: *No combat sport could compare to Jiu Jitsu in terms of efficacy.*

Those who assessed the encounter in good faith - and that was the vast majority - then began to express doubt as to whether *Jiu Jitsu* could take root in France in light of the fact that the Japanese culture was so vastly different from our own.

But French culture is also very far removed from British culture, and yet boxing, which is held in such high esteem in the United Kingdom, was readily assimilated here. It has even come to pass that a master of La Boxe Française defeated an English boxer.

In truth it is simply that *Jiu Jitsu* is unknown, and up until now much has been said of it by those who hardly understand it. In six months to a year... I mean to say that when it becomes a fully *Parisian* thing and everyone is wholly persuaded, first that *Jiu Jitsu* is for everyone, even the French, second that it encompasses the easiest and most practical form of self defense in existence, and third that it is the best of sports. When this happens even the slightest objections to this art since its arrival in our city will have been brushed aside, and in Paris you'll find nothing but partisans of the sport.

To reach this point - and let us hope as quickly as possible, due to the benefits that *Jiu Jitsu* cannot fail to spread through all classes of society since it constitutes the best physical training in the world - it is necessary that everyone show the patience to study it to some extent. Let every citizen move through the excellent preparatory exercises required to enter into this sport.

People also need to come to understand that unlike boxing and wrestling it is not something that calls for a specialized athletic lifestyle and so will only be of use to the initiated: *It is not an art that can only be used to good effect by rare amateurs.*

Such are the errors engendered by hesitation. As with gymnastics and weight training, and more than is the case with fencing, boxing, riding, etc., *Jiu Jitsu* must be made a part of the daily fitness regime of all people who consider themselves health-conscious. It contains within its doctrine all of the best principles of physical culture, and it is within the reach of all, since it does not require the purchase of special equipment in order to be practiced.

In short order every Parisian is going to be doing it.

We are convinced that all of those who give themselves over to penetrating the mysteries of this Japanese art - for in the West we're always wanting to see the mysterious in everything that comes from the East - will understand the immensity of the benefit *Jiu Jitsu* will confer upon them. Everyone will want to avail himself of blessings so conveniently placed at his very doorstep.

Twenty minutes of Jiu Jitsu every morning will render the weak more capable than the strong and able to deal with any attack. As for those who follow the guidelines of hygiene and nutrition found in *Jiu Jitsu* - which are so healthy and uncomplicated - they will not have to wait long to become veritable masters. Perhaps they will even be able to challenge the Japanese masters of that school of physical beauty and superb human health!

II.
History of Jiu Jitsu

Jiu Jitsu can be considered the native wrestling form of Japan, perhaps to the extent of being as indispensable to the Japanese people as rice and cold baths. It is deeply embedded in their culture in the manner of horsemanship among Native Americans and contemplative techniques among the fakirs of India. It is, so to speak, characteristic of the Japanese people, much like the braid which runs down the back of every man in China.

It has been more than two thousand years since Jiu Jitsu, which can be translated as *muscle breaking*, has been introduced into the culture of Japan. For at least five hundred years we are able to follow its development through documentation, tracking its transformation and its perfection through its various teachers, schools, regions and methods.

In the beginning Jiu Jitsu was solely the province of Japanese warriors of that bellicose feudal class which was long the all-powerful master of the nation: The ancient and legendary caste of the *Samurai*. They jealously guarded their secrets in order to maintain dominance over the people.

The portraits and all of the documents which have come down to us from the ancestors of the modern Japanese always show them - like our own warriors of the middle ages - dressed in armor which covers them like a carapace. And always, upon the kakemonos the artists employ to paint their pictures, they are posed like athletes and fighters.

Hence the almost religious reverence with which the Japanese have guarded this sport: It is so closely bound to their venerated ancestors, the primordial heroes of their national history.

When a more democratic spirit melded all of the classes dividing Japanese society into one and the aristocratic spirit was extinguished, the art of self defense which had been the province of the samurai alone rapidly spread among the people - the very population which had marveled at it and been terrorized by it for centuries. In order to gain that same robustness, agility, and capacity to vanquish all enemies, all Japanese became faithful adepts of Jiu Jitsu.

We must not confuse the aristocratic style of Jiu Jitsu with the plebian wrestling form known as sumo - a game of balance and tricks with its professional school based in Osaka.

Sumo wrestlers represent a caste unto themselves which is quite dear to the common people of Japan. They are like heavyweight wrestlers as opposed to the leightweights of western wrestling. The sumo have ever been the popular wrestlers of Japan, even in former times when Jiu Jitsu belonged to the samurai alone.

Their style, which is made up of feats of skill and strength, has a theatrical flavor recalling our own music-hall acrobats or better still our country fair wrestlers.

Today as before Jiu Jitsu can be defined as *the art of combatting and defeating sheer force with speed and skill*. It is thus the safeguard of men of middling strength, the precious and ever-available weapon within the reach of the weak and small to wrestle and defeat those who are larger, stronger, or armed.

I would repeat that no one is too small or too weak to put Jiu Jitsu into practice. Similar sports such as wrestling, boxing, and La Boxe Française - or even savate and la canne - demand great muscular effort, and presuppose the existence thereof. All of that is irrelevant in Jiu Jitsu which is not a matter of *effort* but of *knowledge*.

It is the art of making use of one's flexibility with aplomb, and despite physical weakness, the smallest individual can acquire such suppleness in time. What is most astonishing is that a man of middling strength who practices Jiu Jitsu and knows how to deploy it will always be victorious over any adversary whatsoever, even the strongest of men.

Better still, when we look at other combat sports we see that one is obliged by experience to recognize this truth: Those of moderate strength who remain in the *lightweight* category will never have the chance to defeat an adversary in the *heavyweight* bracket. We learn to accept this truth and will always find it affirmed by experience. On the other hand, a sportsman who comes to Jiu Jitsu immediately discovers the astonishing truth: *The stronger a man who takes on a Jiu Jitsu practitioner is, the more easily he will be beaten.*

There is in Jiu Jitsu, so to speak, an element of prestidigitation. In Japan it has long been understood that the best professors were those who took no account of physical strength and who demanded that their students remove that element from their game: What remains is what is most essential to Jiu Jitsu, which is to say knowing how to retreat and to use "bodily strategy"... To gain advantage over an adversary through that practical anatomical knowledge which will allow one to put the foe out of the fight by turning his strength against him.

This is why Jiu Jitsu has taken such deep root in Japan, a nation of small people who seem to be meager, but who are in fact agile, hardworking, industrious, simple, adroit, and who in a word have just the right attributes for this art to triumph among them. From them we have derived the core principles of Jiu Jitsu which we will now pass on to the reader.

Also, Jiu Jitsu has a national character. It is taught and practiced in schools and universities alongside science and letters. The army and navy impose this discipline upon recruits as we offer our own soldiers courses in military theory. Jiu Jitsu is therefore the logical complement to every young man's education as other sports are in American and English colleges. This is not only because it is the most healthy and useful of exercises, but also because it draws every mind back to a national feeling through all of the associations it carries with the ancestors and chivalry - these are central to the Japanese character.

For the rest, it is a brutal weapon. In a real fight a hold can end in unconsciousness, broken limbs, and sometimes death.

It should be said that some holds are so dangerous that during mere demonstration one can injure a partner unless great care be taken to apply a technique with the greatest prudence and the slowest of movements.

Let us say, in summary, that Jiu Jitsu is the most powerful weapon the weak can use against the strong.

For this reason one witty journalist dubbed it: "An elegant Japanese weapon which allows one to elegantly smash the face of an enemy without our own face being diminished in any way."

And it is beyond doubt that, although it cannot be used in war in the same manner, the physical training imparted through Jiu Jitsu served the Japanese well in their war against Russia. There the soldiers of Mikado proved so stalwart, so full of vigor despite their size, and so *battle ready* that their superiority has not since been questioned.

The sober nature of the Japanese accords perfectly with the Jiu Jitsu regimen, as does their love of baths and their embrace of specialized breathing techniques which aid in the elasticity of the skeletal muscles. Moreover, has sobriety not always gone hand in hand with power?

Rice is widely cultivated in Japan and the crop affords the people a healthy source of energy to such an extent that red meat is reduced to a minimum. They supplement their rice with eggs, fish, fresh vegetables, and above all lettuce. They do not consume bread or potatoes. They are accustomed to eating little and drinking nothing more than water which cleanses the stomach without loading it with deleterious substances, and they drink tea, that marvelous tonic.

All of that prepares their body perfectly for feats of flexibility and agility necessary to Jiu Jitsu. The daily practice of cold baths does for their exterior fortitude what their diet does for their inner health.

Japanese breathing practices add even more to their physical suppleness. There is breathing, and then there is breathing: While every person believes that he is breathing properly, I can assure you that few are breathing with the conscious effort needed to dilate the lungs to their full potential.

For fifteen minutes each morning, Japanese practitioners of Jiu Jitsu breathe according to a reasoned method so as to fill the chest cavity entirely while allowing the stomach to expand, thus ensuring the elasticity of all of the muscles needed for this primary necessity of life.

Only after these exercises are finished do the Japanese begin practicing Jiu Jitsu. They have hit upon an ideal training regime, for not only do they work all of the parts of the body and the four limbs in succession, but they do so without any sort of equipment whatsoever. As when playing a game of cards, all one needs is a partner.

Jiu Jitsu has nothing in common with boxing, it is closer to wrestling. There is no frontal assault aimed at putting the enemy out of the fight with his face streaming blood. The art consists in submitting the opponent without hurting him, making it impossible for him to continue his attack.

All of the poses one can see on Japanese prints depicting Jiu Jitsu are faithful reproductions of the different phases of combat. If these images strike the eye of the western observer as bizarre with their close quarters grappling, it is because the techniques are so different from those found in boxing and wrestling.

Jiu Jitsu consists in exchanging a series of efforts with hand versus hand, chest versus chest, and leg versus leg. The combattants can be seated or even lying down on their backs. Victory goes to the fighter using the more long-range set of tactics, the man playing the longer game, the smarter game, so as to paralyze the foe through the play of limbs before choking him out or snapping a joint.

Now things become dangerous if the losing party fails to concede once taken into a hold, which is why Jiu Jitsu has so long retained its warlike character and its status as a secret science open only to the initiated.

One of the most dangerous strikes used in Jiu Jitsu employs the edge of the hand. Simple training allows one to harden this weapon into a veritable hammer capable of breaking wood or even bone, which could translate into breaking an opponent's forearm, for example.

It is thanks to the exercises found in Jiu Jitsu, along with its rational training system, that the Japanese army, though it may have the smallest soldiers in the world, has the best fighters. All of them are capable of feats of endurance far superior to those of soldiers from other nations. Their use of cold baths inures them to extremes of temperature just as their sobriety and muscular elasticity gives them marvelous resistance in the face of privation, forced marches, and all of the forms of physical suffering that war brings in its train.

For this reason we want Jiu Jitsu to spread quickly. Let it be honored and practiced in France as is already the case in England and America. Since our people are more robust than the Japanese, and French soldiers are more .... nations, the addition of Jiu .... best in the world. It will be .... e illustrious feats our

.... is enough to create
.... e upon this astonishing

.... e an adequate boxer
.... me a fighter to be
.... ‹, no matter how
.... ent. That is the
.... rvation represented

.... his there is no better
.... le passage from the

"La Boxe Française which is so widely practiced in France today is a defensive art, but English boxing and French boxing have become entirely conventionalized. Indeed, if a member of an *Apache* street gang were to attack you, you would not have the opportunity to apprise him of which blows were illegal and which attacks would result in a foul. In the heat of the moment the attacker will seek to use all of his most dangerous weapons *immediately* in order to put his prey out of the fight. He doesn't care about good form or sportsmanship so long as he gets what he came for. The superiority of Jiu Jitsu over boxing becomes striking within the context of street defense: No more conventions or illegal blows, the move that neutralizes the enemy is the best one, and Jiu Jitsu abounds in these. If the attacker throws a punch Jiu Jitsu has wonderful formulas for breaking his forearm, and if he throws a kick his leg is broken. If he is stronger and goes for a bear hug it is no cause for the Jiu Jitsu player to panic: Letting himself fall, the Jiu Jitsu man paralyzes the audacious aggressor. Conclusive experiments have been made in this involving very powerful individuals who knew how to box, wrestle, etc... None were able to resist an adept of Jiu Jitsu for long, even one of average strength. This is why the art is superior to all other means of self defense against any sort of enemy.

"In Jiu Jitsu it is not a question - as with wrestling - of whose shoulders are touching the mat. Indeed most Jiu Jitsu men prefer fighting from their back to any other position when it comes to defeating more powerful adversaries and moving toward the technique which will end the fight.

"Street fighting is real combat without rules and above all without a referee. The adversary is beaten when he cries mercy and, if he should do so with great sincerity, it is because he has been given a reason before which all ill will and pride must vanish: He is in such pain that he is about to pass out."

Through this citation we see how useful this art is for the weak or, if you prefer, for those people who lack strength beyond the average, and how they ought to seek out the doubly healthy sport of Jiu Jitsu.

Here some would perhaps interject that, as in the case of boxing and wrestling, Jiu Jitsu is not for everyone, and that only a handful of elite individuals within a country can practice it with success so as to draw profit from the complex art of Jiu Jitsu.

This is an absolute error which is easily refuted through a moment of reflection. First we have the example of the Japanese who all practice this sport universally, impose it upon their soldiers and encourage it in their schools, and recommend it to their young people just as the Americans nudge their children toward tennis or football. This truth provides evidence that every man can and should practice Jiu Jitsu for the sake of general health, well being, enhanced dexterity, and of course the capacity for self defense.

But let us offer the eight arguments offered by the Japanese school in Paris offered to prove that Jiu Jitsu is for everyone:

1. It can be considered an excellent form of exercise and a means of defense for those who prefer fighting to being beaten.
2. It can be regarded as one of the most noble exercises, imparting courage and self confidence.
3. It is a discipline which can be practiced indoors in an urban setting when an individual does not have easy access to outdoor space.
4. It exercises the body and cultivates the balance in a natural way.
5. It is highly entertaining and a remedy for laziness.
6. A man of little weight has the same chance as the massive man.
7. For women it is at once good exercise and an excellent means of self defense against boors and brutes.
8. For officers of the law and those who frequent areas where strength is the law, Jiu Jitsu is a great means of defending oneself and imposing superiority. From this perspective it can be regarded as the science of combat. In a dark setting it is remarkably efficacious and superior to every other means of defense.

In conclusion it is easy to draw from these arguments the basis of our initial premise: *Jiu Jitsu is the most useful of all sports.*

III.
Preparatory training

All evidence points to this: When you wish to undertake athletic training you must follow a regime, undertake preparatory exercises, and limber up those parts of the body which will come into play in the sport of your choice.

The same is true of Jiu Jitsu. As we have already seen, there is no escaping this general rule. Yet everything the art demands is so natural, so easy to execute and so healthy that to train for Jiu Jitsu is at the same time to give oneself over to the most elementary forms of self-care and hygiene, cleanliness and nutrition.

In France we hear of all sorts of health complaints which multiply by the day among every social class. Through Jiu Jitsu a person becomes as durable and energetic as the Japanese who, having proven their mettle against a European enemy, offer proof of qualities unmatched in our time.

Jiu Jitsu holds within itself a complete and rational system of physical education that is at the same time very easy, as we will see in the preparatory exercises which follow.

The training regimen can be broken down into a few distinct categories:
1. **Nutrition.**
2. **Breathing.**
3. **Hygiene.**
4. **Exercises.**

We shall go through these one by one, formulating the precise rules regarding each point which every European, with a bit of willpower and perseverance, will be able to follow easily without greatly modifying his existing habits or impacting his working life.

1. NUTRITION

Everyone knows that the Japanese are a sober people, and rational sobriety is a key principle in overall health.

The useless foods found on our tables mean that our organism - though perhaps more innately robust than that of the Japanese - is subject to all sorts of maladies which are unknown among the peoples of the Far East!

The rice which forms the basis of Japanese nourishment, boiled in water or steamed, flows easily through the body unlike the potato, and it does not require sharp condiments which are always damaging to the stomach. As it is served in Japan, rice does not resemble our own version of the same. Reduced to a meal it remains agreeable in taste while being healthier, more nutritional, and more fortifying for the body than the best grains we are used to.

Why do we rarely eat it here in France? Why do we tend to prefer the heaviest, hardest to digest foods like beans and potatoes? Would it be so hard to reduce our intake of such sustenance and introduce more rice which is generally avoided here, and yet powers the Japanese military which is known for its feats of endurance in marching? Clearly they have hit upon an energy source which keeps them moving without causing dyspepsia and the like, and is one of the best means of reconstituting the organism.

We also eat very little fish, though our neighbors in England consume quite a lot of it. Now, seafood is one of the cornerstones of Japanese cuisine, and it too offers one of the healthiest, most fortifying forms of nutrition, be it dried, boiled, or served up with sauce.

It seems clear that most Frenchmen would have a hard time eating raw fish in the Japanese fashion, even if it was accompanied by a very lively sauce… But who knows? One could really get used to it. Our stomachs, already battered by overly complicated cuisine, are now awash in pharmaceuticals that are repugnant and foul tasting. A bit of raw fish with some sauce could be neither worse nor more disagreeable to swallow.

Nothing is more delicate than grilled fish, or fish seasoned with some browned butter. But this isn't a course in cookery, and everyone knows there are a thousand ways to prepare seafood. To attain the goal we're setting here, we ask that you simply eat more fish in some form prepared in whatever fashion you please.

As for fruits and vegetables, we do indeed eat those in France - but so few! To begin with, the majority of French people go wild with the spices, and so are put off by the relative blandness of the greens themselves.

In Japan vegetables take second place at the table between rice and fish, and there a twelve hour day is more in vogue among workers than an eight hour day. In fact in France we're already done in after eight hours and seek to shorten the working day whenever possible.

Lettuce, tomatoes, carrots, onions - which the Japanese prefer raw rather than cooked - are the most healthful and nutritive of vegetables, along with radishes and celery.

A Parisian would recoil at the idea of eating a raw onion, but let him take a tour of southern France between Toulouse and Perpignan and see what comprises the meal of the working class down there, especially farmers. He would see how these vigorous folks scarf down many an onion and work from dawn until dusk under the most ardent sun without getting fatigued. The men who built the pyramids ate onions in abundance as well and they accomplished a feat which has yet to be equalled to this day, though we have the advantages of electricity, steam power, and advances in architecture and mechanics at our disposal.

Shall we look at a Japanese menu to get an idea of the practical sobriety of this energetic little nation?

A plate of rice with some grilled fish forms the entree of a man of means - a merchant for example.

Next come the boiled cucumbers with raw onions, followed by a sort of bouillabaisse served in small quantities.

For dessert comes fruit and some cakes made from rice or wheat flour much like our own galettes.

That's all.

Beverages? Would you believe either water or tea, but water above all, and never chilled.

That is a summer menu. In winter they are fortified by extra calories in the form of fish and some hard boiled eggs. Never red meat, and rarely some milk.

That is all that nourishes these vigorous, active, hardworking, and energetic people who know nothing of stomach ailments, dyspepsia, indigestion and intestinal issues. Everyone knows how the Japanese are capable of bearing a load which would crush a European, and that they are inveterate walkers.

Now it is nutrition which provides their muscular power and energy. Let us try their nutritional regime in France - it can be done with a bit of courage. Red meat is not something which fortifies, it is light food which lends power to the body. The people of Asia nourish themselves in this way, and it is beyond argument that they possess the maximum of willpower, energy and vigor.

2. BREATHING

Every living creature must breathe: Plants, fish, amphibians - even us! Now in order to live well, which is to say be healthy and sane, it is quite clear that we must breathe properly.

Whoever has poor respiration - whether the trouble stems from the throat, the thoracic cavity, or defective lungs, or because he lives in an unhealthy area where pollution is great - is threatened with asphyxia, which is to say death.

There is a right and a wrong way to breathe. Poor breathing can be due to the organs themselves or to force of habit, or even the circumstances in which we find ourselves - but this last point is beyond our scope here.

Through a bit of systematic study we can all learn to breathe better.

The anatomical knowledge which is indispensable to Jiu Jitsu has proven to the Japanese that irreproachable respiration trains their lungs for deep breathing, bringing the abdomen into play along with all of the thoracic necessary muscles.

This is why the samurai, the first adepts of Jiu Jitsu, developed special breathing techniques. Upon rising in the morning they would spend fifteen minutes in the open air with hands on thighs, body upright, breathing. Their shoulders would not rise upon inhalation nor fall upon exhalation, allowing the proper muscles their normal play and function.

From this point of view, animals seem much more gifted than human beings, and their instinct compels them - as you will see in examining any quadruped - to breathe normally in the fashion indicated.

We must, therefore, rise up each morning and breathe for fifteen minutes in order to train ourselves and get into the habit: The lungs will be fortified progressively, followed by the organism as a whole.

Deep breathing brings benefits to the heart, regulating palpitations and fostering an even pulse. Excessive inhalation is regulated by another form of breathing which is practiced while lying supine, the arms crossed and the legs spread.

We would add that, in regards to cardiac health, one should at first all exercise and violent activity which gives rise to physiologic excess. Jiu Jitsu is never a matter of forcing something: Remember that it is an exercise in skill requiring ordinary vigor multiplied by the coefficients which are calm and bodily coordination. Instinctive brute force adds nothing to it - quite the contrary.

All of these exercises must be done slowly without haste and without stopping. The strong and the weak will be astonished to find that this daily practice will benefit them immensely once it becomes a habit, following an initial period of fatigue which comes with all new exercises.

Once the stomach is sound from proper nutrition and the thoracic muscles and abdomen have been put in order by regulated breathing which lends to their full play and development, and when the heart is properly regulated by this gymnastics of the chest cavity, we can begin to learn the first principles of Jiu Jitsu.

3. HYGIENE

What if you were to tell a European that before he can learn Jiu Jitsu from a Japanese master, before being taken on as a student and admitted into a school run by professionals, he must first display perfect equanimity, gentleness, submissiveness, politeness, and in short perfect good character?

For those who are astonished at this, consider that Jiu Jitsu includes exceedingly dangerous moves which, when conducted under the influence of anger, can cause the fracturing of a limb, the rupture of muscles, and even death.

That is why adherents of the art must be calm like the Japanese themselves. It must never be that during a match one fails to admit defeat, lest he open the door to serious harm. A student must show the greatest moderation grounded in perfect politeness and good character which are central to the practice of Jiu Jitsu.

After calm, water plays a great role in the hygiene of an adept of Jiu Jitsu. We have already spoken of water as a beverage without hope that a westerner or Parisian would come close to consuming as much as the Japanese - who are known to drink as much as five liters per day.

It is clear that this veritable internal *lavage* cannot help but have a positive effect. I also doubt that any European dares to undertake such a regime.

One absolute rule which must be mentioned is that the Japanese never take their water with ice, whatever the initial temperature might be.

Moreover they don't need iced water due to their practice of taking hot and cold baths. This frees the organism to keep a constant internal temperature while staving off rheumatism - an illness almost unknown in Japan.

The Japanese, even the less fortunate, take two baths per day, sometimes three or more. And do not make the mistake of believing that their frequent hot baths are a mere 30 to 35 degrees celsius! A Frenchman who went to a Japanese bath for the first time would think he was being boiled alive.

The Japanese bathe at all hours of the day in their home courtyards, in full view of passers-by, without any false modesty or shame. But if hot baths are prefered above all by the people of Japan, they do not turn up their noses at cold baths. They take these in winter above all as a sort of tempering agent as soon as they emerge from a hot bath. Some will just go and plunge into a freezing river while others will roll in the snow, then return home to dry off and perhaps have a quick and vigorous massage.

Every town and village in Japan features a public bath, and these are composed of a simple communal pool frequented by both sexes without any shame or modesty attached. Western civilization has done away with this practice in many places with men and women bathing separately.

But in the East the cold bath is king, and hot baths in public establishments find fewer and fewer clients.

This custom of cold dips seems to keep the Japanese from succumbing to heat stroke. They may just duck their heads into a bucket of chill water, or during a hike they will duck their heads in a cold stream, then continue on without drying off in any way.

This system is easy to adopt and uncomplicated - if it does no good, at the very least it causes no harm.

This scrupulous cleanliness causes them to look with contempt upon western cultures with less regard for cleanliness than our own. Those Japanese who dare to say it aloud will opine that we exude a certain odor that they can identify with their eyes closed - and we don't want to encourage this stereotype in the least.

Moreover this phenomenon has given rise to a turn of phrase among the Japanese which is not at all flattering: They say that those who have a bad scent have *the odor of Europeans...*

Clean air also plays its role in Japanese hygiene. In that culture they do have the fear of drafts which causes us such chagrin. Whether it be night or winter, the outer air gives them no cause for fear.

If they have insomnia, they rise up and take a walk.

Even the Japanese wardrobe is open to the wind instead of clinging to the body as is the custom among us. Despite this fact, lung ailments are almost unknown in Japan. Perhaps this is owing to the fact that instead of emptying their sputum into a pocket hanky, they choose to use a square of paper and then throw it away instead of keeping it on their person. Why maintain that which nature has impelled one to discard?

There you have the rules of good hygiene: These are fortifying, easy, and practical, and within the reach of everyone. You don't need to go to Japan to start practicing the rules of health. You can apply them in Paris just as well as in Tokyo.

But you will have to shake up your routine, your habits, the ridiculous conventions of culture, and alas, this can be more difficult than some believe!

That said, let us move on to a series of exercises which strengthen the members and transform the aspirant into a genuine student of Jiu Jitsu.

4. EXERCISES

There are a rather large number of preliminary exercises, and in Japanese schools of Jiu Jitsu students are encouraged to find these themselves insofar as possible so as to properly prepare the muscles of the wrist, arm, and forearm. Never pushing too far, these future scientific wrestlers are strengthened without excessive fatigue.

It is up to the individual to strengthen his wrists by taking one of his hands in the other as if it were that of an adversary, using it to flex his opposite hand and wrist.

One can cross the arms and lean in with the weight of the outside of one forearm on the inside of another. This must be done without raising the arms **(fig. 1)**.

Once you have the habit of these exercises, which are fun as well as beneficial, you should look to extend each session to a length of fifteen minutes each day.

The first, best, and most efficacious exercise recommended by professors of Jiu Jitsu for two people is the following:

Two students stand facing one another at the distance of a meter or so. They clasp both of one another's hands with fingers interlaced and come forward until their chests are touching. Now they both push with arms and chest in such a way as to push one another back a meter or two **(fig. 2)**.

Each repetition of this exercise lasts no more than three minutes, and to begin it should only be repeated three times. This little grappling exercise should cause fatigue, and it conditions the arms, legs, and core while bringing the cardiovascular system into play. With time students will profit greatly from such work.

To work the arms in isolation here are several ideas: To start, two students stand facing and extend their arms toward one another leaning wrist against wrist with the hands balled into a fist. One student now stiffens an arm and in turning around his partner step by step, he tries to displace the opponent's wrist while the man taking the strain endeavors to remain immobile **(fig. 3)**.

The students take turns in this process, each one working the right arm and then the left. Students should work slowly and without violence while bearing in mind the constitution of their partner so as to avoid strain. The muscles of the wrist will become more supple and vigorous through this work.

The same exercise is modified by using the arms themselves: The forearms are bent and the fists remain closed.

One particularly useful exercise focused exclusively on the hands goes as follows: Bring the hands to the height of the belt with the fingers tightly interlaced. One man's hand seeks to twist the opponent's as much as possible against resistance, and students take it by turns to assume the active and resistant role. This works the forearms as well as the wrists.

Two students of Jiu Jitsu can also strive against one another for control of a short stick. Holding it with both hands, one will twist to the right while the other twists to the left in an attempt to pull the baton away from their partner. Once the partners are fatigued on one side, they reverse the direction of pull. All such exercises are for the arms in isolation.

There are other methods for working the legs and ankles: Let each student also work his whole body through hiking and rowing.

The simplest exercises are as follows: Students sit down facing one another with the soles of their feet touching and their arms out behind them supporting the torso. One student pushes his left leg against the other student's foot as hard as he can and raises his opponent's leg from the floor ever so slowly in such a way as to overturn him. This is done in turn by both students with both legs.

In order to work the ankles, students use the same starting position and by turns one will, for example, attempt to thrust the other's leg off to the left. Again, the students will take turns.

One great technique for developing the lumbar and dorsal muscles is to have students stand back to back and take one another's hands with fingers entwined before slowly lifting one another up **(fig. 4)**.

Once these preliminary exercises have been performed in a satisfactory manner we can begin to approach the various attacks and counters of Jiu Jitsu with confidence.

Figure 1

Figure 2

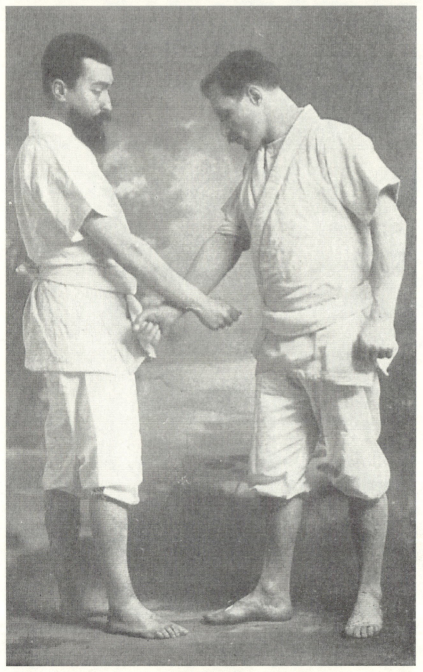
Figure 3

Figure 4

TECHNIQUES

Let's Go!

Figure 5

In wide use among Japanese law enforcement officers, this technique has been baptized *Let's Go!* The move used in isolation is enough to paralyze an opponent.

So soon as you've managed to pass your left arm over the right attacking arm of your assailant, hold fast to his right wrist with your right hand. With your left arm pressed tight to your body, bring his right wrist to you with your left hand. With your left forearm under his elbow, grip your right wrist with your left hand. Having clinched this lock, the more you squeeze your hands to your body the more chance the enemy's arm has of being dislocated at the elbow. The pain he will experience will bring him to submission.

Twist the Hand

Figure 6

Seize the opponent's attacking hand and, with a simple twist which is well applied, throw him to the ground and reduce him to submission.

The success of this move relies upon applying both of your thumbs to his metacarpals just where the fingers begin so as to create the longest possible lever. Now twist the hand in on the forearm and away from his body relative to the shoulder of his trapped hand. A little pressure is enough to send him down.

The opponent's hand cannot be grabbed with both of yours at the same time: First snatch his left with your right, and vice versa.

When applied quickly this move is certain to succeed.

Send him over your head

Figure 7

Grab the adversary by his collar with both hands and put your foot on his stomach. Leap so as to send your other leg between those of your opponent insofar as possible. At the same time tug his collar toward you as you fall backwards, dragging him along.

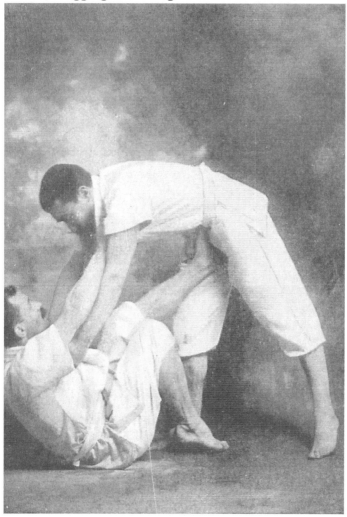

Figure 8

Extend the leg which has been applied to his abdomen in order to launch your adversary. He is obliged to fall, and then you should follow up in the manner to be indicated.

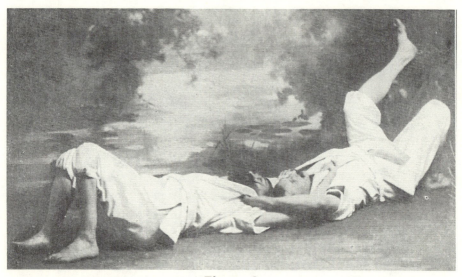

Figure 9

With the opponent flat on his back, maintain your grips and drive your hips skyward as you pull at his vestment.

Figure 10

This brings you to a mounted position on top of the opponent.

Figure 11

At this point you have a number of options. The first is to set a knee on one of his arms and maintain the other with your opposite foot which you will set on his wrist.

Your right hand seizes his collar at the back, gripping as close to the nape of his neck as possible. Your left hand also grabs his collar, but this grip is not as deep, and you use this hand to pull his garment. Your right forearm is a lever which induces strangulation.

Figure 12

Another technique involves snagging his left wrist with your left hand, bending his arm, and introducing your right forearm through the crook of his elbow. Apply your right fist to his left wrist and lever it such that the joint is forced backwards.

Counter a choke

Figure 13

If the attacker reaches to grab you by the throat, fade back with your upper body as you slap his wrists against one another, then send his arms up over your head.

Figure 14

Release his left wrist and seize his right in both hands. Pass your left elbow over his arm while maintaining control of the wrist.

As his arm is being twisted he is forced to bend forward at the hips. His chest comes to your hip and he finds himself immobilized, defenseless due to the pain.

Counter a high knife attack.

Figure 15

When menaced with a high-to-low knife attack, use your forearm to block the attacker's descending forearm.

Figure 16

Now use your right hand to secure his right wrist and step forward with your left foot, passing your left hand behind the attacking forearm. Grab your own right wrist.

At this point you must cinch down on the lock you have just created in order to disarm the attacker.

Figure 17

Here we see another response to the same attack: Having secured the opponent's wrist and moving to the lock shown in **figure 16**, place the palm of your left hand on the opponent's elbow. Raise his elbow up as you lever his trapped wrist down beneath it, and your attacker will be obliged to bow. Pass his arm over your forearm and straighten it such that his shoulder becomes the fulcrum, then grab the attacker by the throat with your right hand. His elbow is against your chest. All you have to do is raise his forearm to produce pain in his shoulder - a truly terrible lock.

Counter a knife attack II

Figure 18

Let us say that you are in your left guard, which is to say your left hand is your lead hand. The assailant comes at you with the knife in his right hand, moving it from high to low. Block his forearm with your own left forearm and apply the lock with your right arm after the manner explained in **figure 16**.

Counter a leg kick

Figure 19

    The assailant stands in left guard and throws a kick (the low kick, point kick, or *chasse*). Force his attacking leg from left to right with your lead leg, in this case the left.

Figure 20

    Now use a drop-step, launching forward off of your right leg so as to impact the attacker's chest with your left shoulder. At the same time you must sweep the back of his leg with your own left leg. If you happen to be standing in right guard, these instructions are reversed.

Counter a punch

Figure 21

When a straight punch aimed at your face comes in, slip your head to the side and pass under the assailant's arm. Trap his free hand in order to stop a bodyblow. Now bring him down with a sweep.

Arm lock

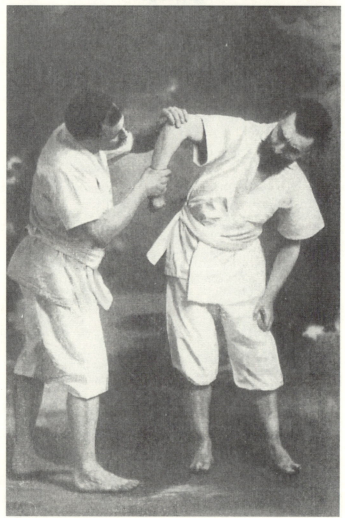

Figure 22

Arm locks are the most common offensive tools. Here is one such technique: When a punch comes in, instead of slipping your head as indicated above, issue a forearm block in the manner shown for the counter-knife technique **(fig. 16, 17).**

Pass under the attacking arm

Figure 23

If you manage to seize the opponent's wrist, cinch your grip and yank his arm so as to unbalance him. This will keep him from striking as you pass under his trapped arm.

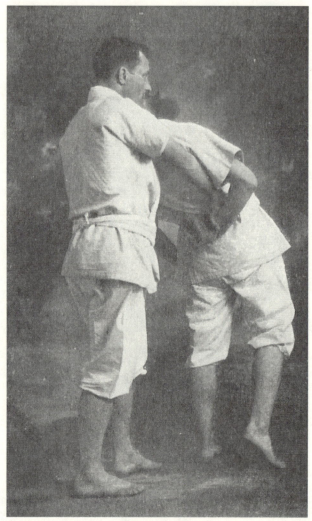

Figure 24

Once under his arm - the right arm, for example, as per **figure 22** - your right hand maintains his wrist while your left goes to his hand. Apply a thumb to his metacarpals and twist. Your adversary will be forced to offer you his back and expose his throat which can then be seized in the manner shown in **figure 28**.

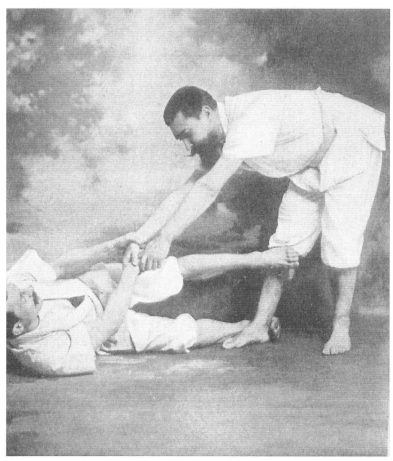

Figure 25

In this figure the man who is standing has passed under the arm of the opponent as described above. The counter to this technique is as follows: When the adversary has passed under your arm, roll to the mat in the direction of the torsion being applied. Now the wrist hold becomes the point of departure for a counterattack aimed at his legs.

In this figure the right leg is attacked. Notice that you will be on your right side. Your bottom foot hooks the back of his heel while your top foot goes behind his knee to yank it forward. As your adversary stumbles you should snatch his right wrist which will have relinquished its hold upon you.

Invert the hand

Figure 26

If the opponent reaches for you with his right arm, snag the attacking hand with your left hand and place your thumb at the extremity of his metacarpals. Raise his arm and place the thumb of your right hand beside your left thumb. Force the opponent's wrist back onto his forearm and outward at the same time. The man thus seized cannot resist. If he tries anything, he risks a broken wrist and being sent to the ground.

Another arm lock

Figure 27

If an adversary should bring your arm to his body, free yourself by passing your left arm under his right tricep so as to keep his wrist in your armpit. Place your right hand on his anterior deltoid while grabbing your own right wrist with your left hand which has been passed under the attacker's right arm. Use your right hand to shove his deltoid from inside to outside and turn on your own axis to give him your back if you are smaller than he is. Your adversary will be compelled by pain to rise up on his toes, and he will not be able to strike you. **Note: In all locks involving the elbow, your fulcrum is located at several centimeters above the joint.**

Strangulation

Figure 28

Having turned aside a punch or a knife thrust, displace the aggressor with your free arm such that you cause him to make a half turn.

Now that you are behind him, pass your left forearm (for example) across his throat while you snag his right arm with your own, turning him such that you have his back. Apply your foot to the back of his knee to destroy his base.

Attack the cervical vertebrae

Figure 29

You've brought the opponent down and have attempted to apply a forearm choke. The adversary grabs both of your wrists to stymie your efforts: Profit from this position by forcing his head down using your chest while applying your forearm as if to flatten his body to the floor. This is a more dangerous move than the prior one, and it requires more practice.

Grounded armbar

Figure 30

Once you've unbalanced the opponent, throw yourself on him and apply this lock which will finish him - most of the time. He will be looking to grab your throat: This is the ideal setup for this technique.

Grab one of his wrists with both hands, choosing the one that coincides to the side you happen to be laying on. Alternatively, if you happen to be mounted on the opponent, fall to the side you choose. Pass a leg over the neck of your opponent to set your foot on the opponent's other wrist. Use your other leg to keep the adversary from raising his hips.

Pull his target arm to you and, while maintaining tight control of his other arm with your foot, arch your back. This is one of the most common techniques used in Jiu Jitsu.

Strangle with vertebral separation

Figure 31

Whether it be during a standing grapple or a scramble on the ground, whenever the opponent presents his back you should pass your forearm across his throat, overhook his legs with your own, and set a heel on each of his thighs.

Cinch all of these holds tightly before arching into him forcefully. This is a very dangerous move which can produce death by strangulation or through the separation of vertebrae.

Toe hold

Figure 32

In this figure the attacker has immobilized the left leg of his opponent with a lock. He seizes the toes of the right foot with his right hand and shoves against the heel with his left hand. This allows him to elongate the attacked leg fully.

Now turn the foot inward. Sinking this lock requires the total immobilization of the opponent, otherwise he will roll on his axis and avoid the effect of the torsion entirely.

Break the elbow with a knee

Figure 33

If you are able to put a knee on the opponent's back near to the armpit, seize his arm and set his tricep on that same knee. Use it as a fulcrum as you force his forearm backwards.

With your free hand render him fully immobile by shoving his chin to the mat, or failing that, you can force his neck down.

Break the elbow with your instep

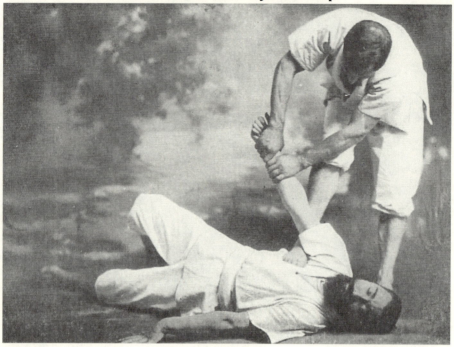

Figure 34

This obtains the same result as the prior technique if, after taking the adversary down through a wrist lock, you set your foot beneath his armpit on the same side as his trapped arm. Now as you squash the adversary to the mat, use the instep as you did the knee, setting the tricep against it as you wrench the elbow.

Achilles lock

Figure 35

The opponent is supine and attempts to employ his feet defensively. Scoop his right foot with your left arm such that the toes are trapped in your armpit. Send your left forearm under his achilles' tendon. At the same time set your right palm on the inside of his trapped leg and drape the fingers over the shin. Grab your right forearm with your underhooking left hand and cinch your holds on toes, shin, and tendon. As you come to a stand the crushing pressure on his achilles' tendon will force submission.

Break the neck

Figure 36

Your opponent is supine. Your left hip traps his right arm and your right leg is over him, immobilizing his left arm. Place your left hand on the top of his skull and your right under his chin. Twist his neck away from his trapped right arm.

Once the twist is complete, put a hand on the nape of his neck to force his head to his chest. This is a fatal technique.

This technique presents itself in either direction: If the receiving party is laying on your left arm, immobilize him with your left leg and right arm. Place your right hand atop his head and your left on his chin, then twist the head from left to right.

END.

Manufactured by Amazon.ca
Acheson, AB